D1455829

# TEAM SPIRIT ®

## SMART BOOKS FOR YOUNG FANS

# THE CLEVELAND BROWNS

## BY
## MARK STEWART

NORWOOD HOUSE PRESS

CHICAGO, ILLINOIS

Norwood House Press
P.O. Box 316598
Chicago, Illinois 60631

For information regarding Norwood House Press, please visit our website at:
www.norwoodhousepress.com or call 866-565-2900.

All photos courtesy of Getty Images except the following:
Icon SMI (4, 12), Black Book Partners (6, 19, 30, 37, 43 both), Author's Collection (9, 16, 33, 41),
Pro/NFL Properties, Inc. (10), Topps, Inc. (11, 15, 17, 18, 23, 34 right, 36, 42 top),
General Mills (20), Cleveland Browns/NFL (22, 35 top left & bottom), TCMA Ltd. (27, 34 left, 38),
Philadelphia Chewing Gum Co. (28), Exhibit Supply Co. (31), Pacific Trading Cards (35 top right),
Sunoco, Inc. (39), Bowman Gum Co. (40, 45), JBC (42 bottom), Matt Richman (48).
Cover Photo: Icon SMI

The memorabilia and artifacts pictured in this book are presented for educational and informational purposes,
and come from the collection of the author.

Editor: Mike Kennedy
Designer: Ron Jaffe
Project Management: Black Book Partners, LLC.
Special thanks to Topps, Inc.

Library of Congress Cataloging-in-Publication Data

Stewart, Mark, 1960-
    The Cleveland Browns / by Mark Stewart.
       p. cm. -- (Team spirit)
    Includes bibliographical references and index.
    Summary: "A revised Team Spirit Football edition featuring the Cleveland
Browns that chronicles the history and accomplishments of the team. Includes
access to the Team Spirit website which provides additional information and
photos"--Provided by publisher.
    ISBN 978-1-59953-519-7 (library edition : alk. paper) -- ISBN
978-1-60357-461-7 (ebook)
    1. Cleveland Browns (Football team : 1946-1995)--Juvenile literature. 2.
Cleveland Browns (Football team : 1999- )--History--Juvenile literature.  I.
Title.
    GV956.C6S74 2012
    796.332'640977132--dc23
                                             2012014327

Manufactured in the United States of America in North Mankato, Minnesota.
205N—082012

**COVER PHOTO**: The Browns are greeted by their fans as they jog onto the field.

# Table of Contents

| CHAPTER | PAGE |
|---|---|
| Meet the Browns | 4 |
| Glory Days | 6 |
| Home Turf | 12 |
| Dressed for Success | 14 |
| We Won! | 16 |
| Go-To Guys | 20 |
| Calling the Shots | 24 |
| One Great Day | 26 |
| Legend Has It | 28 |
| It Really Happened | 30 |
| Team Spirit | 32 |
| Timeline | 34 |
| Fun Facts | 36 |
| Talking Football | 38 |
| Great Debates | 40 |
| For the Record | 42 |
| Pinpoints | 44 |
| Glossary | 46 |
| Overtime | 47 |
| Index | 48 |

**ABOUT OUR GLOSSARY**

In this book, there may be several words that you are reading for the first time. Some are sports words, some are new vocabulary words, and some are familiar words that are used in an unusual way. All of these words are defined on page 46. Throughout the book, sports words appear in **bold type**. Regular vocabulary words appear in ***bold italic type***.

# Meet the Browns

**B**eing the new kid on the block is never easy. The Cleveland Browns have been the new kids three times. They were one of the first members of a new league in the 1940s, and then the newest member of an old league in the 1950s. Finally, they were a brand-new team in 1999. Through it all, the Browns have been one of the most beloved teams in sports.

The Browns come from the part of America where *professional* football got its start. They still win games the old-fashioned way. Cleveland players tackle and block with all their might, and they never give up. Cleveland fans expect nothing less.

This book tells the story of the Browns. It is a tale of two teams, both old and new. Throughout their history, the Browns have shown what great coaches and players can accomplish when they work together. They have also proved that the success of one team can change the game.

Here come the Browns! The Cleveland defense prides itself on making game-changing plays.

# Glory Days

**F**ootball has a long and glorious history in Ohio. Years before the **National Football League (NFL)** began, the top pro teams in the country played there. The best football was not played in the big cities but in the small towns. In fact, the city of Cleveland did not have its first champion until 1945. That year, in their eighth and final season there, the Rams won the NFL title. However, Cleveland fans did not have much time to celebrate. In 1946, the Rams moved to Los Angeles, California.

That same year, a new football league started. The **All-America Football Conference (AAFC)** placed teams in cities where the NFL did not play. Cleveland was an easy choice. Picking a coach was easy, too. Paul Brown understood how football was changing. He knew that the game would get faster and more complicated. There would be more passing and many different types of defenses. Brown was so well respected that the team was actually named after him!

Brown went out and found a group of players whose skills would be perfect for his new brand of football. Several of these players were African Americans, including Marion Motley. They had been barred from the NFL since the 1930s. Motley helped the Browns become the best team in the AAFC. Other Cleveland stars included quarterback Otto Graham and kicker Lou Groza. The team won the championship each year from 1946 to 1949 and lost a total of four games during those seasons.

After the 1949 season, the Browns, San Francisco 49ers, and Baltimore Colts were invited to join the NFL. Cleveland won its **conference** each year from 1950 through 1955 and again in 1957. The Browns took the NFL championship three times during this period.

The Browns had great talent during the 1950s. Graham, Motley, and Groza were still team leaders. The roster featured

**LEFT**: Paul Brown talks with some of his players during the 1950s.
**ABOVE**: Otto Graham prepares to fire a pass.

many other **All-Pro** players, including Bill Willis, Frank Gatski, Mike McCormack, Don Colo, Len Ford, Don Paul, Dante Lavelli, Horace Gillom, Ray Renfro, Mac Speedie, and Dub Jones.

Season after season, Cleveland found ways to stay a step ahead of the competition. Brown was the first to make his players study game film every week. He

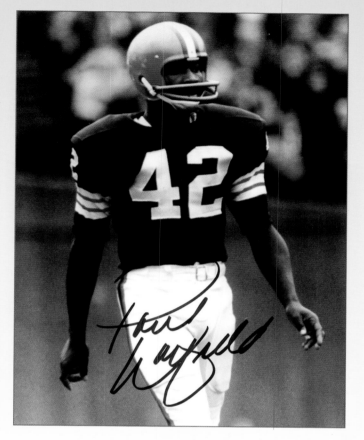

also hired a full staff of assistant coaches to help him. No one had done that before. Brown had a great eye for talent. He could look at a player and see exactly how he would fit into the team's system.

A new *era* began when the Browns **drafted** running back Jim Brown. He played from 1957 to 1965 and led the NFL in rushing every year but one. In 1964, Brown helped Cleveland win another NFL championship. His talented teammates included receivers Paul Warfield and Gary Collins and quarterback Frank Ryan.

**LEFT**: Jim Brown runs the ball against the New York Giants.
**ABOVE**: Paul Warfield was a star on the 1964 team.

Over the next 30 years, the Browns put many more good players on the field, including Leroy Kelly, Jerry Sherk, Don Cockroft, Brian Sipe, Greg Pruitt, Joe DeLamielleure, Ozzie Newsome, Matt Bahr, Bernie Kosar, and Michael Dean Perry. However, the team was unable to win the NFL championship again.

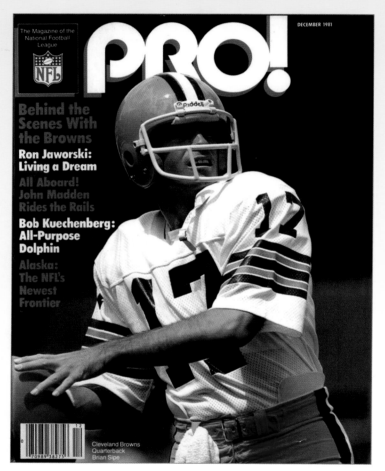

The Magazine of the National Football League

**PRO!**

DECEMBER 1981

NFL

**Behind the Scenes With the Browns**

**Ron Jaworski: Living a Dream**

**All Aboard! John Madden Rides the Rails**

**Bob Kuechenberg: All-Purpose Dolphin**

**Alaska: The NFL's Newest Frontier**

Cleveland Browns Quarterback Brian Sipe

In 1995, team owner Art Modell stunned fans when he announced plans to move the Browns to Baltimore, Maryland. The team would eventually become the Ravens. The NFL promised Cleveland a new team that would carry on its *tradition* and history.

In 1999, Cleveland fans got the team they were promised. The new Browns started from scratch. They found unwanted players from other NFL clubs and then rounded out their roster with college players. Their first coach was Chris Palmer. Their first stars were quarterback Tim Couch, receiver

Kevin Johnson, defensive lineman Keith McKenzie, and linebacker Jamir Miller.

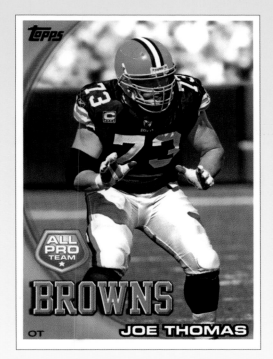

The Browns played in a new stadium, but the old energy and excitement filled the building every Sunday. Cleveland fans knew they had to be patient. While they waited for the team to improve, they had fun bringing back many traditions from the past. In just their fourth season, the Browns went 9–7 and won a **Wild Card** spot in the **playoffs**. It was a true team effort. Not a single player on the Browns was named All-Pro or even picked to play in the **Pro Bowl**.

In the years that followed, the Browns continued to add talent to their roster. Josh Cribbs, Braylon Edwards, Joe Thomas, Shaun Rogers, and D'Qwell Jackson ranked among the top players at their positions. They helped form a good foundation for young stars such as running back Trent Richardson and quarterbacks Colt McCoy and Brandon Weeden. Through their ups and downs, the Browns have stayed focused on building a team that can compete for a championship.

**LEFT**: Brian Sipe's passing was front-page news in the 1970s and 1980s.
**ABOVE**: This trading card shows Joe Thomas protecting the quarterback.

# Home Turf

Since their first season in the AAFC in 1946, the Browns have played on the shore of Lake Erie. Their first home was Cleveland Municipal Stadium. It could get very cold there on windy winter days. The Browns didn't mind it. They liked having that as part of their home-field advantage.

In 1999, the team opened Cleveland Browns Stadium. It brought back wonderful memories for many fans. The new stadium was built on the same piece of land as the old stadium. The field runs in the exact same direction. The famous "Dawg Pound" is still located on the east side of the stadium. Fans dressed as dogs sit there and bark out their support for the Browns.

## BY THE NUMBERS

- The Browns' stadium has 73,200 seats.
- The stadium is 933 feet wide, 695 feet long, and 171 feet high.
- The scoreboards can show animation in 16.7 million shades of colors.

The Browns' stadium is right in the heart of Cleveland.

# Dressed for Success

The Browns haven't made many changes to their look over the years. Their colors are orange, white, and—what else?—brown. Their helmets are orange with two brown stripes and one white stripe running down the middle. In some seasons during the 1940s and 1950s, white helmets were used. In other years, player numbers were added to the sides of the helmets.

When Paul Brown was the coach, the team *logo* was a "brownie" holding a football and wearing a crown. A brownie is a tiny elf-like creature. The Cleveland brownie has never appeared on the team's helmet.

**Frank RYAN**
CLEVE. BROWNS • Q'BACK

The logo was "retired" after Art Modell bought the team in 1962. Even so, the brownie continued to pop up here and there as the team's *mascot*. In 2005, he began appearing on team gear and souvenirs. Fans were glad to have him back.

**LEFT**: Colt McCoy wears the team's road uniform during a 2011 game.
**RIGHT**: Frank Ryan models the team's home uniform from the 1960s.

# We Won!

When the Browns joined the AAFC in 1946, they quickly proved they were the best team in the new league. Cleveland won its first seven games and finished the year with a 12–2 record.

MARION MOTLEY
FULLBACK-CLEVELAND BROWNS
6'1" - 238 lbs.

Chosen fullback on the All-Conference team for three years

In the **AAFC Championship Game** that season, the Browns played the New York Yankees. Otto Graham passed Cleveland to a 14–9 lead. In the fourth quarter, the Yankees were driving for the winning score when Graham—who also played defense—**intercepted** a pass to secure victory for the Browns.

In 1948, Cleveland went 14–0 during the regular season—including wins in

CLEVELAND BROWNS

three road games in eight days during November! They played the Buffalo Bills for the championship and destroyed them 49–7. Marion Motley was unstoppable. He ran for 133 yards and scored three touchdowns. The team's perfect 15–0 record would not be equalled for 24 years.

The Browns won their fourth and final AAFC crown in 1949. A year later, the Browns became part of the NFL. Some predicted that Cleveland would struggle against tougher competition, but the Browns proved them wrong. They finished 10–2 in the regular season, and then defeated the New York Giants and Los Angeles Rams in the playoffs to become NFL champions. The Rams actually led the title game by one point late in the fourth quarter, but Lou Groza kicked a **field goal** with 28 seconds left for a 30–28 victory.

Cleveland played for the NFL championship again each year from 1951 to 1955. After losses in their first three attempts, the Browns rolled over the Detroit Lions in the 1954 title game, 56–10.

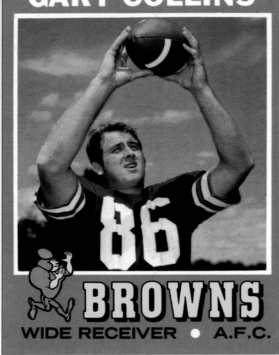

**GARY COLLINS**
**86**
**BROWNS**
WIDE RECEIVER • A.F.C.

Graham, who announced that this would be his last game, scored three touchdowns.

Coach Paul Brown begged Graham to come back for one more year. The quarterback agreed to return for the 1955 season. No one was surprised when Graham led the team to a 9–2–1 record and its 10th appearance in the championship game in 10 seasons.

The Browns faced the Rams again. The Cleveland defense intercepted three passes in the first half and shut down the Los Angeles attack. In the second half, Graham threw for one touchdown and ran for two more. His performance helped turn a close game into an easy 38–14 victory.

Cleveland rebuilt around Jim Brown in the late 1950s, and Blanton Collier replaced Paul Brown as head coach in 1963. In 1964, the Browns played for the NFL championship once again, this time against the Baltimore Colts. The Cleveland defense **shut out** Baltimore, and Gary Collins caught three touchdown passes from Frank Ryan in an amazing 27–0 victory.

The Browns returned to the **NFL Championship Game** twice more in the 1960s, but they lost both times. In 1970, the Browns, Colts, and Pittsburgh Steelers joined the NFL's **American Football Conference (AFC)**. It took a while for the Browns to become one of the AFC's top teams.

Cleveland had excellent teams in 1986 and 1987. Coach Marty Schottenheimer guided the Browns from the sidelines, and quarterback Bernie Kosar was the leader on the field. The Browns had an excellent defense that created lots of problems for opponents. Cleveland fans eagerly awaited a trip to the Super Bowl. Unfortunately, the Browns lost the AFC championship in both seasons to the Denver Broncos.

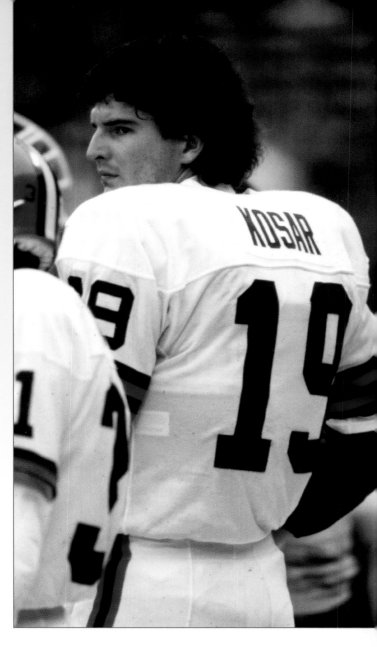

**LEFT**: Gary Collins
**ABOVE**: Bernie Kosar

# Go-To Guys

To be a true star in the NFL, you need more than fast feet and a big body. You have to be a "go-to guy"—someone the coach wants on the field at the end of a big game. Browns fans have had a lot to cheer about over the years, including these great stars ...

## THE PIONEERS

OTTO GRAHAM
QUARTERBACK, CLEVELAND BROWNS

### OTTO GRAHAM                           Quarterback

- BORN: 12/6/1921    • DIED: 12/17/2003
- PLAYED FOR TEAM: 1946 TO 1955

Otto Graham was a great passer, a powerful runner, and a *dynamic* leader. He always seemed to find a way to win. Graham was the **Most Valuable Player (MVP)** twice in the AAFC and twice again in the NFL.

### MARION MOTLEY                         Running Back

- BORN: 6/5/1920   • DIED: 6/27/1999   • PLAYED FOR TEAM: 1946 TO 1953

Marion Motley was one of football's first "big backs." He was a fast runner and a great blocker. When Otto Graham dropped back to pass, Motley made sure no one laid a hand on him.

## LOU GROZA — Kicker/Lineman

- BORN: 1/25/1924 • DIED: 11/29/2000
- PLAYED FOR TEAM: 1946 TO 1959 & 1961 TO 1967

Lou Groza was nicknamed "The Toe" because he was such a talented and powerful kicker. He also played on the offensive line for Cleveland for 14 years. Groza was voted into the **Hall of Fame** in 1974.

## BILL WILLIS — Lineman

- BORN: 10/5/1921
- PLAYED FOR TEAM: 1946 TO 1953

Bill Willis was the key to Cleveland's great defense. When he lined up in the center of the team's five-man line, opponents did not dare run plays up the middle.

## JIM BROWN — Running Back

- BORN: 2/17/1936 • PLAYED FOR TEAM: 1957 TO 1965

Many football experts consider Jim Brown the greatest runner in NFL history. He was bigger than most linebackers and had the speed of a sprinter. It usually took two or three tacklers to bring Brown down. He averaged more than five yards every time he touched the ball.

## GENE HICKERSON — Offensive Lineman

- BORN: 2/13/1935 • DIED: 10/20/2008 • PLAYED FOR TEAM: 1958 TO 1973

Gene Hickerson worked with Dick Schafrath to open big holes for Cleveland runners. Hickerson was a powerful blocker at the **line of scrimmage**, but he was also quick enough to lead sweeps around the end.

**LEFT**: Otto Graham     **ABOVE**: Bill Willis

### GREG PRUITT                                    Running Back

• BORN: 8/18/1951    • PLAYED FOR TEAM: 1973 TO 1981

When the Browns drafted Greg Pruitt, they viewed him as a part-time player. After a few seasons, Cleveland didn't want to take him off the field. In 1975, Pruitt gained nearly 2,000 yards in **total offense** and scored 10 touchowns.

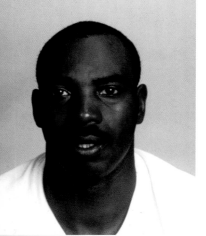

### BRIAN SIPE                                     Quarterback

• BORN: 8/8/1949    • PLAYED FOR TEAM: 1974 TO 1983

Brian Sipe was a great passer and respected leader. He battled through injuries to become one of the best quarterbacks in the NFL. Sipe led the league in touchdown passes in 1979 and was the MVP in 1980.

### OZZIE NEWSOME                                  Tight End

• BORN: 3/16/1956    • PLAYED FOR TEAM: 1978 TO 1990

Ozzie Newsome was too big to be a wide receiver, so the Browns made him a tight end. He was a good blocker and a great receiver. During one stretch of his career, Newsome caught at least one pass in 150 games in a row.

### MICHAEL DEAN PERRY                             Defensive Lineman

• BORN: 8/27/1965    • PLAYED FOR TEAM: 1988 TO 1994

Michael Dean Perry was a fierce tackler who made opponents worry on every play. Perry was named All-Pro twice. His brother William "The Refrigerator" Perry was also an NFL star.

## BERNIE KOSAR · Quarterback

- BORN: 11/25/1963 · PLAYED FOR TEAM: 1985 TO 1993

Bernie Kosar threw the ball with a strange slingshot motion, but he was a very accurate passer. He was also a tough competitor who hated to lose. After Kosar retired, he became a business leader in Cleveland and helped bring a new team to the city.

## JOSH CRIBBS · Receiver/Returner

- BORN: 6/9/1983
- FIRST YEAR WITH TEAM: 2007

Few players were as fun to watch as Josh Cribbs. Every time he touched the ball, he had a chance to reach the end zone. In his first seven seasons in Cleveland, he returned 11 kicks for touchdowns. In 2009, Cribbs was named an All-Pro.

## JOE THOMAS · Offensive Lineman

- BORN: 12/4/1984 · FIRST YEAR WITH TEAM: 2007

Joe Thomas weighed more than 300 pounds, but he moved with great **agility**. He was picked to play in the Pro Bowl in each of his first five seasons as a Brown. The only other Cleveland player to do that was Jim Brown. Thomas was runner-up in the **Rookie** of the Year voting in 2007.

**LEFT**: Ozzie Newsome
**ABOVE**: Josh Cribbs

# Calling the Shots

A coach has to be pretty good for a team to name itself after him. Paul Brown was known around Ohio as a brilliant high school coach in the 1930s. In the 1940s, he proved himself at Ohio State University. During World War II, he coached powerful teams made up of soldiers at the Great Lakes Naval Training Station.

After Brown was hired to coach Cleveland's new team in 1946, he reached out to players he had known in high school, college, and the military. They all jumped at the chance to play for him. Several of these players were African Americans. During the 1930s and 1940s, pro football teams ignored people of color. Brown didn't agree with this unwritten rule. He built his teams with the best players he could find.

The offense that Brown ran in Cleveland relied on the run and the pass. It was similar to offenses used by all NFL teams today. Back then, it was considered very modern. He was one of the first coaches to call plays from the sideline. Brown would send a new lineman into the huddle on each down to let quarterback Otto Graham know what to do.

Paul Brown gets a ride from his players after winning the 1950 championship.

Brown might have continued coaching the team forever. In 1961, however, Art Modell became the new owner. Modell liked to do things his way, and he replaced Brown with Blanton Collier. The new coach was very popular. He let his players have more say in the way the team was run. Collier led the Browns to the NFL title game four times from 1964 to 1969.

Following the success of Brown and Collier wasn't easy. The Browns looked for leaders who could guide them back to the top of the football world. They found talented coaches in Sam Rutigliano, Marty Schottenheimer, Forrest Gregg, Bill Belichick, and Romeo Crenell. Unfortunately, none of them were able to produce a championship.

# One Great Day

During Cleveland's early years, the team's fans got used to winning championships. From 1946 to 1957, the Browns played for the league title 11 times and won seven of them. However, in the six seasons that followed, Cleveland came up short again and again. Finally, in 1964, the team returned to the NFL Championship Game.

That was the good news. The bad news was that the Browns faced the Baltimore Colts. Baltimore's roster was loaded with stars, including Lenny Moore, Raymond Berry, and Johnny Unitas. The Colts brought the NFL's most powerful offense to Cleveland two days after Christmas. The fans at Municipal Stadium hoped for the best.

The Browns knew they had a good offense of their own. Frank Ryan was a top quarterback, Gary Collins and Paul Warfield were excellent receivers, Lou Groza was a great kicker, and Jim Brown was the best running back in football. Cleveland also had talented linemen on offense and defense. In fact, the Browns would win the battle "in the trenches" all day long.

The game opened with 30 minutes of scoreless football. Cleveland got on the board first with a field goal by Groza in the third quarter. The Browns added 14 more points on two touchdown catches by Collins. Groza kicked a second field goal in the fourth quarter, and Collins caught his third scoring pass.

Baltimore, meanwhile, could not move the ball. The Cleveland defense pressured the Colts all day long. Linebacker Galen Fiss seemed to be everywhere, making tackles all over the field. When the game ended, the Browns were NFL champions with a 27–0 victory. For Cleveland fans, life was back to normal.

# Legend Has It

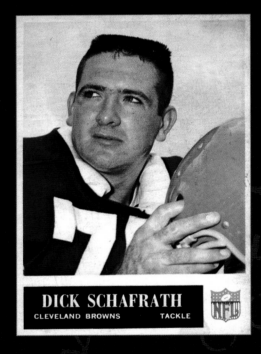

**DICK SCHAFRATH**
CLEVELAND BROWNS          TACKLE

## Did the first person to cross Lake Erie in a canoe play for the Browns?

**LEGEND HAS IT** that he did. Lineman Dick Schafrath was known for never backing down from a challenge. He once jogged more than 60 miles from Cleveland to his hometown on a dare. He also wrestled a bear and won several eating contests. When Schafrath heard that no one had ever canoed across Lake Erie, he couldn't believe it. He grabbed a paddle, pushed off from shore, and crossed the lake. Today, people attempt the same daring trip every spring and summer.

**ABOVE**: Dick Schafrath

# Who was the best last-round pick in the history of the NFL draft?

**LEGEND HAS IT** that Warren Lahr was. Lahr was taken by the Pittsburgh Steelers in the 32nd and last round of the 1947 draft. But he hurt his knee and was cut before he played a game. Paul Brown thought the Steelers made a mistake and signed Lahr. He became one of the league's best pass defenders. Lahr had 44 interceptions for the Browns and was voted All-Pro six times.

# Did the Browns have the first "taxi squad" in professional football?

**LEGEND HAS IT** that they did. A taxi squad refers to the group of players who aren't on a team's active roster. They get a chance to suit up for a game if there is an injury. The term came about because Cleveland's first owner, Art McBride, owned several taxi companies in the city. When a player was cut, McBride gave him a job driving one of his taxis. When the Browns needed a player to fill in, he simply rejoined the team.

When Cleveland joined the NFL in 1950, many people believed that the team would struggle to win games. The Browns were eager to prove their critics wrong. Cleveland's first game provided the perfect opportunity to do that. The Browns faced the Philadelphia Eagles. Philadelphia had won the league championship in 1949.

Everyone expected a blowout, and they got one. But it was the Browns who rolled to victory, 35–10. Cleveland's first three touchdowns came on passes by Otto Graham. He scored the fourth touchdown himself, and the final score came on a 57-yard run by Dub Jones.

LEFT: Otto Graham
RIGHT: Marion Motley

Coach Paul Brown felt satisfied. The Browns had shown they were as good as any team in the NFL. But he still did not get all the respect he deserved. After the game, a Philadelphia coach said, "Brown would have made a better basketball coach because all they do is put the ball in the air."

Eleven weeks later, the Browns and Eagles met again in Philadelphia. The Browns won 13–7, without completing a single pass. Graham handed the ball to Jones and Marion Motley all day, and the Eagles couldn't stop them. Meanwhile, the defense shut down the Philadelphia offense. Brown had made his point—again!

After the game, the Browns boarded a plane for their flight back to Cleveland. When the pilot asked the control tower if it was okay to leave, the players could hear the response: "You're clear for takeoff … get those Browns out of town!"

# Team Spirit

Cleveland fans cherish loyalty and tradition. They rooted for the Rams from 1937 to 1945, until the team moved to Los Angeles. They rooted for the old Browns from 1946 to 1995, until the team moved to Baltimore. When the new Browns played their first season in 1999, more than 70,000 fans bought tickets for the first **preseason** game.

The seats behind the east end zone of the Browns' stadium are reserved for the Dawg Pound. During the 1980s, defensive backs Hanford Dixon and Frank Minnifield began calling themselves "Big Dawg" and "Little Dawg." Fans began showing up to games dressed as dogs to show their support. Soon everyone in one section started calling themselves the Dawg Pound. When Cleveland players score a touchdown, they often jump into the stands there to celebrate.

**LEFT**: Quincy Morgan enters the Dawg Pound. He was the team's best receiver in 2002.    **ABOVE**: This pin was made with the hope that the Browns would win the 1986 AFC championship. They fell just short.

T he Browns have had a lot to celebrate over the years. This timeline shows some of the greatest moments in team history.

**1946**
The Browns play their first AAFC season.

**1964**
The Browns win their fourth NFL championship.

**1950**
The Browns win their first NFL championship.

**1957**
Jim Brown is voted Rookie of the Year and MVP.

**1968**
Leroy Kelly wins his second NFL rushing title in a row.

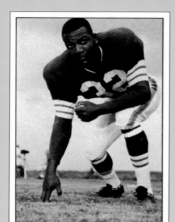

Jim Brown

Leroy Kelly

LeRoy
**KELLY**
CLEVE. BROWNS • RUNNING BACK

Jerry
Sherk

Tim Couch was
a leader of the
2002 team.

**1976**
Jerry Sherk is
named AFC Defensive
Player of the Year.

**1999**
The Browns
rejoin the NFL.

**2002**
The Browns return
to the playoffs.

**1972**
Don Cockroft leads the
NFL in punting yards and
**field goal percentage**.

**1987**
The Browns
reach the AFC
Championship Game.

**2009**
Josh Cribbs returns
three kickoffs for
touchdowns.

Don
Cockroft

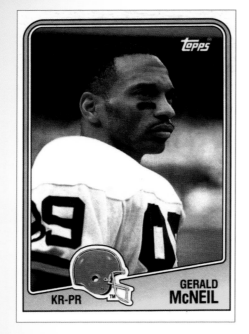

GERALD
McNEIL

KR-PR

### LIGHT YEARS

When Gerald McNeil played for the Browns, he was one of the NFL's top punt returners. He was also the lightest player in the league. McNeil stood 5′ 7″ and weighed just 140 pounds.

### SLAM-DUNK QUARTERBACK

Before Otto Graham joined the Browns, he played professional basketball for the Rochester Royals. They were champions in the 1945–46 season.

### WHAT'S IN A NAME?

The Browns have had some of the coolest names in the NFL over the years. Included on the list are Mac Speedie, Pio Sagapolutele, and Ebenezer Ekuban.

**ABOVE**: Gerald McNeil    **RIGHT**: Dante Lavelli

## STUCK LIKE GLUE

Dante Lavelli caught 386 passes for the Browns in the 1940s and 1950s. He almost never dropped a ball. His teammates nicknamed him "Gluefingers."

## A GREAT RUN

After nine years in the NFL, Jim Brown decided to retire and focus on his acting career. Cleveland fans were shocked when the bruising back announced that his playing

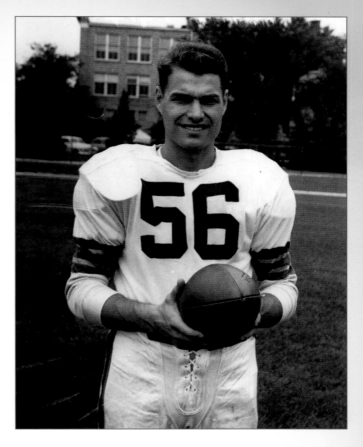

days were over. But the Browns did not skip a beat. Leroy Kelly took over for Brown and led the NFL in touchdowns three years in a row. He was the league's top rusher in 1967 and 1968.

## BRAINIAC

Frank Ryan was the quarterback of the Browns when they won the 1964 NFL championship. He might have been the smartest player in the league. Ryan studied *physics* in college and earned a *Ph.D.* in mathematics.

"He was a special guy. He was the spirit of the Cleveland Browns."
► **Mike McCormack,** *on Lou Groza*

"As long as the ball got there on time, it didn't matter how it looked."
► **Bernie Kosar,** *on his sometimes wobbly passes*

"The test of a quarterback is where his team finishes. By that standard, Otto Graham was the best of all time."
► **Paul Brown,** *on his star quarterback*

"My attitude and my competitiveness will not let me fail."
► **Joe Thomas,** *on what made him one of the NFL's top linemen*

"It meant a lot that he paved the way and showed that guys of our color could play and that we were **disciplined**. I'm very appreciative for him."

▶ **Braylon Edwards,** *on Bill Willis*

"Few people could do what Gene accomplished during his career. He **personified** the great tradition of the Cleveland Browns."

▶ **Dante Lavelli,** *on Hall of Famer Gene Hickerson*

**66 Gene Hickerson RG**
**Cleveland Browns**

"The game we have today can be traced back to the many things he started doing in the 1950s."

▶ **Art Modell,** *on Paul Brown*

"I don't have any trophies in my home on display. I don't claim to be the best at anything."

▶ **Jim Brown,** *on letting his accomplishments speak for themselves*

**LEFT**: Mike McCormack
**ABOVE**: Gene Hickerson

# Great Debates

**P**eople who root for the Browns love to compare their favorite moments, teams, and players. Some debates have been going on for years! How would you settle these classic football arguments?

### Lou Groza had the most powerful leg on the Browns ...

... because the record books say so. For 14 years, The Toe kicked field goals and played on the offensive line for Cleveland. When Groza retired as a lineman, he came back as a kicker for seven more seasons. Groza had legs like tree trunks and loved to attempt field goals with the game on the line. Today, the NFL's best kicker is given the Lou Groza Award.

HORACE GILLOM

### Groza had the best toe. But Horace Gillom had the strongest leg ....

... because no one in football could punt the ball higher or farther. Fans "oohed" and "aahhed" in the stands whenever Gillom (LEFT) kicked the ball. By the time one of his punts came down, opponents had almost no chance to return it. Gillom averaged almost 46 yards per punt. That was the team record for 50 years!

## The Cleveland teams of the AAFC would have beaten the 1964 Browns ....

... because they had great players at every position. Otto Graham was football's best passer, Marion Motley was the game's most powerful runner, and Mac Speedie (RIGHT) and Dante Lavelli were tremendous receivers. The Cleveland defense was also excellent. The 1964 Browns simply would not be able to stop Graham and his teammates head-to-head.

MAC SPEEDIE
End - Cleveland Browns
6'3" - 205 lbs.
Specially noted for his skill on "hook" passes

## No way! The 1964 Browns would find a way to defeat those guys ....

... because they played their best against the toughest competition. In the 1964 NFL title game, the mighty Baltimore Colts could not score a single point. Cleveland's offense was just as good as the defense. Jim Brown ran like a runaway freight train. Receivers Paul Warfield and Gary Collins combined for 17 touchdowns. Leroy Kelly was the league's most dangerous kick returner. The 1964 Browns were unstoppable on both sides of the ball.

# For the Record

The great Browns teams and players have left their marks on the record books. These are the "best of the best" …

Brian Sipe

Michael Dean
Perry

## BROWNS AWARD WINNERS

| WINNER | AWARD | YEAR |
|---|---|---|
| Otto Graham | AAFC Most Valuable Player | 1947 |
| Otto Graham | AAFC Most Valuable Player | 1948 |
| Paul Brown | AAFC Coach of the Year | 1949 |
| Otto Graham | NFL Most Valuable Player | 1951 |
| Paul Brown | NFL Coach of the Year | 1951 |
| Otto Graham | NFL Most Valuable Player | 1953 |
| Paul Brown | NFL Coach of the Year | 1953 |
| Lou Groza | NFL Most Valuable Player | 1954 |
| Otto Graham | NFL Most Valuable Player | 1955 |
| Jim Brown | NFL Rookie of the Year | 1957 |
| Jim Brown | NFL Most Valuable Player | 1957 |
| Paul Brown | NFL Coach of the Year | 1957 |
| Jim Brown | NFL Player of the Year | 1965 |
| Jerry Sherk | AFC Defensive Player of the Year | 1976 |
| Forrest Gregg | NFL Coach of the Year | 1976 |
| Brian Sipe | NFL Most Valuable Player | 1980 |
| Michael Dean Perry | AFC Defensive Player of the Year | 1989 |

# BROWNS ACHIEVEMENTS

| ACHIEVEMENT | YEAR |
|---|---|
| Western Conference Champions | 1946 |
| AAFC Champions | 1946 |
| Western Conference Champions | 1947 |
| AAFC Champions | 1947 |
| Western Conference Champions | 1948 |
| AAFC Champions | 1948 |
| AAFC Champions | 1949 |
| Eastern Conference Champions | 1950 |
| NFL Champions | 1950 |
| Eastern Conference Champions | 1951 |
| Eastern Conference Champions | 1952 |
| Eastern Conference Champions | 1953 |
| Eastern Conference Champions | 1954 |
| NFL Champions | 1954 |
| Eastern Conference Champions | 1955 |
| NFL Champions | 1955 |
| Eastern Conference Champions | 1957 |
| Eastern Conference Champions | 1964 |
| NFL Champions | 1964 |
| Eastern Conference Champions | 1965 |
| Century Division Champions | 1967* |
| Century Division Champions | 1968 |
| Century Division Champions | 1969 |
| AFC Central Champions | 1971 |
| AFC Central Champions | 1980 |
| AFC Central Champions | 1985 |
| AFC Central Champions | 1986 |
| AFC Central Champions | 1987 |
| AFC Central Champions | 1989 |

*From 1967 to 1969, the NFL had four divisions. The Century Division included the Browns, New York Giants, St. Louis Cardinals, and Pittsburgh Steelers.*

**ABOVE**: Sam Rutigliano coached the 1980 team. **BELOW**: Joe DeLamielleure was a star on the 1980 team.

# Pinpoints

The history of a football team is made up of many smaller stories. These stories take place all over the map—not just in the city a team calls "home." Match the pushpins on these maps to the **Team Facts**, and you will begin to see the story of the Browns unfold!

# TEAM FACTS

**1** Cleveland, Ohio—*The Browns started playing here in 1946.*

**2** Bronx, New York—*The Browns won the 1947 AAFC championship here.*

**3** Los Angeles, California—*The Browns won the 1950 and 1955 NFL championships here.*

**4** Brookfield, Wisconsin—*Joe Thomas was born here.*

**5** Philadelphia, Pennsylvania—*Leroy Kelly was born here.*

**6** Hobbs, New Mexico—*Colt McCoy was born here.*

**7** Pensacola, Florida—*Trent Richardson was born here.*

**8** St. Simons Island, Georgia—*Jim Brown was born here.*

**9** Farmington, West Virginia—*Frank Gatski was born here.*

**10** Fort Worth, Texas—*Frank Ryan was born here.*

**11** American Samoa—*Pio Sagapolutele was born here.*

**12** Accra, Ghana—*Ebenezer Ekuban was born here.*

Frank Gatski

# Glossary

🧠 Football Words
🧠 Vocabulary Words

**AAFC CHAMPIONSHIP GAME**—The game that decided the league champion.

*AGILITY*—The ability to move quickly and easily.

**ALL-AMERICA FOOTBALL CONFERENCE (AAFC)**—The professional league that played for four seasons, from 1946 to 1949.

**ALL-PRO**—An honor given to the best players at their positions at the end of each season.

**AMERICAN FOOTBALL CONFERENCE (AFC)**—One of two groups of teams that make up the NFL. The winner of the AFC plays the winner of the National Football Conference (NFC) in the Super Bowl.

**CONFERENCE**—A group of teams that play against each other.

*DISCIPLINED*—Serious and precise.

**DRAFTED**—Chosen from a group of the best college players. The NFL draft is held each spring.

*DYNAMIC*—Exciting and energetic.

*ERA*—A period of time in history.

**FIELD GOAL**—A goal from the field, kicked over the crossbar and between the goal posts. A field goal is worth three points.

**FIELD GOAL PERCENTAGE**—A statistic that measures a kicker's success on field goal attempts.

**HALL OF FAME**—The museum in Canton, Ohio, where football's greatest players are honored.

**INTERCEPTED**—Caught in the air by a defensive player.

**LINE OF SCRIMMAGE**—The imaginary line that separates the offense and defense before each play begins.

*LOGO*—A symbol or design that represents a company or team.

*MASCOT*—An animal or person believed to bring a group good luck.

**MOST VALUABLE PLAYER (MVP)**—The award given each year to the league's best player; also given to the best player in the Super Bowl and Pro Bowl.

**NATIONAL FOOTBALL LEAGUE (NFL)**—The league that started in 1920 and is still operating today.

**NFL CHAMPIONSHIP GAME**—The game played to decide the winner of the league each year from 1933 to 1969.

*PERSONIFIED*—Represented a quality in human form.

*PH.D*—The highest honor in education.

*PHYSICS*—The area of science covering matter and energy.

**PLAYOFFS**—The games played after the regular season to determine which teams play in the Super Bowl.

**PRESEASON**—Before the regular season.

**PRO BOWL**—The NFL's all-star game, played after the regular season.

*PROFESSIONAL*—Paid to play.

**ROOKIE**—A player in his first season.

**SHUT OUT**—Did not allow an opponent to score.

**TOTAL OFFENSE**—Rushing yards plus receiving yards plus return yards.

*TRADITION*—A belief or custom that is handed down from generation to generation.

**WILD CARD**—A team that makes the playoffs without winning its division.

# OVERTIME

**TEAM SPIRIT** introduces a great way to stay up to date with your team! Visit our **OVERTIME** link and get connected to the latest and greatest updates. **OVERTIME** serves as a young reader's ticket to an exclusive web page—with more stories, fun facts, team records, and photos of the Browns. Content is updated during and after each season. The **OVERTIME** feature also enables readers to send comments and letters to the author! Log onto:

**www.norwoodhousepress.com/library.aspx**
and click on the tab: **TEAM SPIRIT** to access **OVERTIME**.

Read all the books in the series to learn more about professional sports. For a complete listing of the baseball, basketball, football, and hockey teams in the **TEAM SPIRIT** series, visit our website at:

**www.norwoodhousepress.com/library.aspx**

## On the Road

**CLEVELAND BROWNS**
100 Alfred Lerner Way
Cleveland, Ohio 44114
440-891-5000
www.clevelandbrowns.com

**THE PRO FOOTBALL HALL OF FAME**
2121 George Halas Drive NW
Canton, Ohio 44708
330-456-8207
www.profootballhof.com

## On the Bookshelf

To learn more about the sport of football, look for these books at your library or bookstore:

* Frederick, Shane. *The Best of Everything Football Book.* North Mankato, Minnesota: Capstone Press, 2011.

* Jacobs, Greg. *The Everything Kids' Football Book: The All-Time Greats, Legendary Teams, Today's Superstars—And Tips on Playing Like a Pro.* Avon, Massachusetts: Adams Media Corporation, 2010.

* Editors of *Sports Illustrated for Kids. 1st and 10: Top 10 Lists of Everything in Football.* New York, New York: Sports Illustrated Books, 2011.

# Index

PAGE NUMBERS IN **BOLD** REFER TO ILLUSTRATIONS.

Bahr, Matt.........................10
Belichick, Bill...................25
Berry, Raymond..................26
Brown, Jim....................**8**, 9, 18,
21, 23, 27, 34,
**34**, 37, 39, 41, 42, 45
Brown, Paul....................6, **6**, 7, 9,
15, 18, 24, 25, **25**,
29, 30, 31, 38, 39, 42
Cockroft, Don.................10, 35, **35**
Collier, Blanton...............18, 25
Collins, Gary.............9, 18, **18**, 27, 41
Colo, Don...........................9
Couch, Tim....................10, **35**
Crenell, Romeo..................25
Cribbs, Josh.............11, 23, **23**, 35
DeLamielleure, Joe............10, **43**
Dixon, Hanford...................33
Edwards, Braylon..............11, 39
Ekuban, Ebenezer..............36, 45
Fiss, Galen.....................27, **27**
Ford, Len...........................9
Gatski, Frank...............9, 45, **45**
Gillom, Horace..............9, 40, **40**
Graham, Otto...............7, **7**, 16,
18, 20, **20**, 24,
30, **30**, 31, 36, 38, 41, 42
Gregg, Forrest.................25, 42
Groza, Lou...................7, 17, 21,
**26**, 27, 38, 40, 42
Hickerson, Gene............21, 39, **39**
Jackson, D'Qwell................11
Johnson, Kevin...................11
Jones, Dub...................9, 30, 31
Kelly, Leroy.......10, 34, **34**, 37, 41, 45
Kosar, Bernie..........10, 19, **19**, 23, 38

Lahr, Warren.....................29
Lavelli, Dante.........9, 37, **37**, 39, 41
McBride, Art......................29
McCormack, Mike...........9, 38, **38**
McCoy, Colt.................11, **14**, 45
McKenzie, Keith..................11
McNeil, Gerald...............36, **36**
Miller, Jamir....................11
Minnifield, Frank................33
Modell, Art...............10, 15, 25, 39
Moore, Lenny....................26
Morgan, Quincy...................**32**
Motley, Marion.............7, **16**, 17,
20, 31, **31**, 41
Newsome, Ozzie.............10, 22, **22**
Palmer, Chris....................10
Paul, Don..........................9
Perry, Michael Dean.......10, 22, 42, **42**
Perry, William...................22
Pruitt, Greg.................10, 22
Renfro, Ray........................9
Richardson, Trent.............11, 45
Rogers, Shaun....................11
Rutigliano, Sam...............25, **43**
Ryan, Frank........9, **15**, 18, 27, 37, 45
Sagapolutele, Pio.............36, 45
Schafrath, Dick............21, 28, **28**
Schottenheimer, Marty.........19, 25
Sherk, Jerry...........10, 35, **35**, 42
Sipe, Brian...........10, **10**, 22, 42, **42**
Speedie, Mac.............9, 36, 41, **41**
Thomas, Joe.........11, **11**, 23, 38, 45
Unitas, Johnny...................26
Warfield, Paul...........9, **9**, 27, 41
Weeden, Brandon.................11
Willis, Bill.............9, 21, **21**, 39

## About the Author

**MARK STEWART** has written more than 50 books on football and over 150 sports books for kids. He grew up in New York City during the 1960s rooting for the Giants and Jets, and was lucky enough to meet players from both teams. Mark comes from a family of writers. His grandfather was Sunday Editor of *The New York Times,* and his mother was Articles Editor of *Ladies' Home Journal* and *McCall's*. Mark has profiled hundreds of athletes over the past 25 years. He has also written several books about his native New York and New Jersey, his home today. Mark is a graduate of Duke University, with a degree in history. He lives and works in a home overlooking Sandy Hook, New Jersey. You can contact Mark through the Norwood House Press website.